FORGET-ME-KNOT
by
DAVID TRISTRAM

JULIA ZEINFELD
INSPECTOR MONROE
ROBERT
SAMANTHA

A Flying Ducks Publication

You'll find more information on Flying Ducks Publications on our webbed site:

www.davidtristram.playwright.com
e-mail: davidtristram@playwright.com

ISBN 1 900997 03 7

Flying Ducks Publications, Station Road, Highley, Shropshire, WV16 6NW

ACT ONE

A telephone rings in a spotlight. It is eventually answered by a very tetchy Julia, who emerges fastening a dressing gown. On the opposite side of the stage, another spotlight picks out Inspector Monroe, who is making the call.

Julia All right, all right, I'm coming. Yes?

Monroe Mrs Zeinfeld?

Julia Yes.

Monroe Mrs Julia Zeinfeld?

Julia Who is this?

Monroe Mrs Zeinfeld, it's Detective Inspector Monroe, Leicester CID.

Julia Police?

Monroe Sorry to trouble you so early, Mrs Zeinfeld. Look, it's nothing to be too concerned about...

Julia *(prompted by Monroe's comment, she checks the time on her watch)* It's six o'clock in the morning!

Monroe I realize that, but I thought you ought to know.

Julia Know what?

Monroe Mrs Zeinfeld - I think we've found your husband.

Julia I didn't know I'd lost him.

Monroe *(deflated)* Oh. Is your husband there at the moment, Mrs Zeinfeld?

Julia My husband is away on business. He's not due back until Saturday. Look, what the hell's going on?

Monroe Bear with me, Mrs Zeinfeld. Could you describe your husband please?

Julia Yes, he's a two-timing bastard - why?

Monroe I mean what does he look like?

A Flying Ducks Publication

Julia He looks like a two-timing bastard.
Monroe Please, Mrs Zeinfeld.
Julia Are you serious?
Monroe Very.
Julia He's tall - about 6 feet 2 - thin - short dark hair...
Monroe Right, well, I think you'll find he's actually here with us.
Julia Where?
Monroe In Leicester.
Julia Leicester? What the bloody hell's he doing in Leicester? He's supposed to be in Blackpool.
Monroe Mrs Zeinfeld, your husband was picked up by one of my officers early this morning. At first we thought he'd been drinking.
Julia He doesn't drink.
Monroe No, well, we let the doctor have a quick look at him and, well, it seems he's suffering from amnesia.
Julia Amnesia?
Monroe Loss of memory.
Julia I know what bloody amnesia means!
Monroe He appears to have suffered a slight blow to the head - nothing too serious - but he can't seem to remember...well, he can't seem to remember anything, actually.
Julia Look, if this is some kind of office wind-up, I'm...
Monroe It's not a joke, Mrs Zeinfeld, I can assure you. I think you should get over here as soon as possible.
Julia Over where?
Monroe Leicester.
Julia That's bloody miles away.
Monroe I can't help that, Mrs Zeinfeld.
Julia Look, when you say he can't remember anything...
Monroe I mean he can't remember anything. He can't explain what he was doing in Leicester, how he got there, his address...
Julia This is ridiculous! I mean Robert's a dopey sod at the best of times but even he can remember his own address!
Monroe Mrs Zeinfeld! He doesn't even know his own name. He doesn't know who he is.
Julia Christ.

Monroe All we know about him is what's in his filofax. We need you up here.
Julia Where are you?
Monroe Leicester Police Station. Right opposite the Town Hall.
Julia *(a resigned sigh)* I'll be there tomorrow afternoon.

She slams the phone down on a bemused Monroe.

Monroe Don't rush yourself.

The spotlight fades on Monroe.

Julia What the bloody hell's he doing in Leicester?

The spotlight fades on Julia.

The spotlight fades back up on Monroe's office. It is the following morning. He enters, fiddling with a portable phone – hastily keying in numbers and listening - trying to crack the pin number code. We hear the results amplified.

"Welcome to Orange answerphone. Please enter your pin number, followed by the hash key. Five, nine, two, four is not a valid pin number. Seven, one, two, nine is not a valid pin number. Eight, three one, nine, seven, two, four, four, four, nine, six, nine, seven, one, seven, seven, seven seven is not a valid..."

There's then the sound of the battery dying on the phone. Monroe curses.

Monroe Bollocks! *(He picks up his office phone and punches an internal number. There's no answer. The phone can be heard ringing just outside his door. Irritated, he flings open the door of his office, and shouts)* Answer the bloody phone, George! *(He slams the door and goes back to pick up the phone. After two more rings, the outside phone stops)* Thank you. George, I want you to get me a charger for a Nokia...nk502. It's a phone, George. I don't know where from! Try the shop on the corner. Well of course not the bloody vegetable shop! The one on the other corner! Yes, George, well, that's why I'm in here and you're out there!

A Flying Ducks Publication

He slams his phone down and starts fiddling with the mobile again. His desk phone rings again almost immediately. Momentarily confused, he answers the mobile, before realizing it's the other phone that's ringing.

Monroe Monroe? About bloody time. All right, send her in.

Monroe goes to the door and opens it, just as an angry Mrs Zeinfeld enters.

Monroe Mrs Zeinfeld... *(He holds out a hand of greeting, which is ignored)*
Julia Where the hell are you supposed to park in this shithole?
Monroe ...welcome to Leicester.
Julia Twenty-five minutes I've been driving around this nightmare city.
Monroe It can be a bit awkward. It's the one-way system.
Julia Yes. One way to hell.
Monroe I presume you found somewhere eventually.
Julia Damn right. On the pavement in front of your building.
Monroe *(with a sigh, he picks up the phone and punches in the internal number)* What sort of car is it?
Julia Mercedes sports. Convertible.

Again he jumps up in irritation that the phone isn't being answered. Just as he opens the door to scream, the phone stops. Monroe slams the door defiantly and stomps back to the phone.

Monroe George - there's a Mercedes sports parked outside. Make sure it doesn't get clamped, will you? Well get it off! Thank you. Oh, and don't try that again, all right? That business with the phone. You know what I mean - you do it on purpose. Yeah, well there's going to be some changes around here, George, you mark my words. *(He slams the phone down once, and then again several times, as if going through the motions of clubbing George. This out of his system, he switches back to an air of polite calm)* Right, Mrs Zeinfeld, let's get the formalities out of the way first. Do you recognize these? *(He holds up a bunch of keys)*
Julia They're his.

A Flying Ducks Publication

Monroe And the filofax?

Julia Yes, this is Robert's all right. 5th March. "Got up. Cleaned teeth." The man just oozes charisma. One of the perks of being an accountant.

Monroe So, this is your husband.

Julia There's no need to rub it in.

Monroe Oh, and is this his mobile?

Julia Looks like it.

Monroe Do you know the pin number?

Julia I don't even know the phone number. I never ring him. Why?

Monroe There's a message on it. I thought it might help give us a clue about what happened. *(The latter half of the sentence is obscured by Monroe voraciously chomping on a sandwich)*

Julia What?

Monroe I said it might give us a clue about what happened.

Julia What's that in your mouth?

Monroe My lunch.

Julia It does nothing for your diction.

Monroe Do you know the pin number or not?

Julia No.

Monroe It's usually a four number sequence.

Julia Well, knowing the extent of my husband's creative imagination, I'd try 1,2,3,4.

Monroe Tried it.

Julia First four numbers of the phone number?

Monroe Tried that as well.

Julia Birthday?

Monroe Nope.

Julia God knows. Why don't you ask him?

Monroe Given that he's struggling to remember his own name, I thought I might be pushing my luck. *(Offering her a sandwich)* Egg and cress?

Julia No, thank you.

Monroe No, well, you wouldn't, would you.

Julia What's that supposed to mean?

Monroe I couldn't help noticing your address.

Julia What about it?

A Flying Ducks Publication

Monroe Wentworth Estate. Very nice. Not exactly back-to-back slums around there, are they? More canapés than sarnés I'd imagine.

Julia Don't worry, I won't be applying for legal aid.

Monroe Eagle View. Let me think now, that's the big white building with the green roof, overlooking the golf course.

Julia How did you know that?

Monroe Oh, believe it or not, that used to be my patch. I was a DC over your way for six years.

Julia *(totally unimpressed)* Really?

Monroe Yeah. Small world, eh?

Julia Small but dull.

Monroe I got transferred here two weeks ago.

Julia What did you do? Murder the Chief Inspector?

Monroe Promotion.

Julia Wentworth to Leicester. Interesting definition of promotion.

Monroe Unusual name, Zeinfeld. Wouldn't have any connection with Zeinfeld Publishing, by any chance?

Julia Yes. But then somehow I think you already knew that.

Monroe There's some serious cash in pornography, then.

Julia It is not pornography.

Monroe It certainly makes an obscene amount of money.

Julia There's nothing more obscene than a jealous policeman.

Monroe So, Victor Zeinfeld would be...

Julia My father.

Monroe Your father?

Julia Yes.

Monroe Not father-in-law.

Julia Correct.

Monroe Isn't it more usual to adopt your husband's surname when you get married?

Julia Not when your name is Zeinfeld and his name is Smith.

Monroe I see. Well, I'll go and fetch him, shall I?

Julia Can't you keep him?

Monroe Reading between the lines, I'd say you two don't get along too well.

Julia You should be a detective.

Monroe Look, I haven't told him you're here. The doc said some sort of visual stimulus could help jolt the memory back to life. I think it's better if I just wheel him in, and we'll see what happens - okay?

Julia Oh, I'll stimulate him all right.

Monroe There is just one thing. I'm er...I'm not sure how to put this.

Julia Put what?

Monroe Has your husband ever done any acting?

Julia Acting?

Monroe Local am-dram - anything like that?

Julia Inspector, the most creative thing my husband ever did was spill gravy down his tie. Why do you ask?

Monroe Well, I'll be honest with you, Mrs Zeinfeld.

Julia An honest policeman. There's a novelty.

Monroe I'm not totally convinced about this amnesia business.

Julia What do you mean?

Monroe Has anything like this ever happened to him before?

Julia What - loss of memory? Oh, yes - birthdays, anniversaries, happens all the time.

Monroe But to forget everything like that - the doctor reckons it's very unusual.

Julia You said he'd had a blow to the head.

Monroe Yes, but even so.

Julia So, what are you saying? That he's just pretending he's lost his memory?

Monroe It's a possibility.

Julia Why would he want to do that?

Monroe I was hoping you could tell me.

Julia Sorry.

Monroe Oh well, maybe I'm just a cynical old copper.

Julia I think that's the more likely explanation.

Monroe I'll go get him. Just do me a favour would you? Just till we sort out what's what - leave all the talking to me.

Julia You're the policeman.

Monroe exits, and re-enters a few moments later with Robert Zeinfeld.

Monroe Robert, there's someone I'd like you to meet.

A Flying Ducks Publication

Robert How do you do.

Mrs Zeinfeld stares at him, quizzically. Monroe takes Robert to one side and they exchange comments in a confidential half whisper.

Monroe Well?
Robert Well what?
Monroe Do you recognize this lady?
Robert Should I?
Monroe Do you?
Robert Should I?
Monroe Do you?
Robert No!
Monroe Are you sure?
Robert Yes.
Monroe Well you should.
Robert Who is she?
Monroe It's Mrs Zeinfeld.
Robert *(unimpressed)* Terrific.
Monroe It's your wife.
Robert *(suddenly screaming out loud)* My wife??
Monroe I'm afraid so.
Julia Thanks a bunch!
Monroe No, I didn't mean it like that...
Robert *(pointing)* But this woman...*(he takes Monroe to one side and lowers his voice)*...this woman means nothing to me!
Monroe That's not unusual with wives.
Julia Inspector...
Monroe Please, Mrs Zeinfeld. Leave this to me.
Robert I need to talk to you - in private - now!
Monroe All right, come with me.
Julia Inspector!
Monroe *(to Mrs Zeinfeld)* I'll be back.

A Flying Ducks Publication

They exit, leaving a worried-looking Mrs Zeinfeld staring into space. She suddenly snaps out of her trance, pulls out a mobile phone, and dials a number.

Julia Benny? Benny, it's Julia Zeinfeld. Listen, I'd like you to do me a big favour...

The lights fade on that side of the stage and back up on the other as Monroe and Robert enter in animated discussion.

Robert Inspector, that is not my wife.
Monroe How do you know?
Robert She's not my type.
Monroe Wives never are.
Robert I'm telling you - I would not marry that woman.
Monroe So what is your type?
Robert I don't know. But it's not that. She's too...aggressive.
Monroe She never said a word!
Robert She looks too aggressive.
Monroe She's also very rich.
Robert That's hardly relevant. How rich?

Monroe has found a chocolate, which again mangles his diction.

Monroe She drives a Mercedes.
Robert What?
Monroe She drives a Mercedes.
Robert A Mercedes?
Monroe *(still enjoying the chocolate)* Mmm.
Robert What sort is it?
Monroe Truffle.
Robert A Mercedes truffle?
Monroe Mercedes sports. Convertible. And she lives in a huge house on the Wentworth Estate. Her father is Victor Zeinfeld - a millionaire publisher. You still say she's not your wife?
Robert I'll keep an open mind.

Monroe Look, you have Mr Zeinfeld's filofax, Mr Zeinfeld's mobile, Mr Zeinfeld's keys. Mrs Zeinfeld described you in detail, to me, over the phone, before she even arrived here. Now, she's identified you in person. I don't really think there's really any more doubt about your identity. You are Mr Robert Zeinfeld!

Robert So you say.

Monroe So she says.

Robert And so say all of us.

Monroe You are Mr Robert Zeinfeld, and the woman in there, like her or hate her, is your extremely rich wife!

Robert I don't hate her, I just don't know her!

Monroe Your memory will return.

Robert Great. Then maybe I'll remember that I hate her.

Monroe You might remember that you love her.

Robert I doubt it.

Monroe Why?

Robert Because she's not my type.

Monroe I think we're going round in circles.

Robert Are you married?

Monroe Yes.

Robert Is she your type?

Monroe God knows. I hardly ever see her.

Robert Oh. You're separated.

Monroe Only by careers.

Robert What?

Monroe She's a doctor. I'm a copper. We occasionally meet when someone's been stabbed. I was hoping to have half an hour with her tonight, but then you show up.

Robert Do you love her?

Monroe *(taken aback)* What?

Robert Do you love your wife?

Monroe *(embarrassed)* Shut up!

Robert Not nice, is it? Having someone poke around inside your emotions.

Monroe Oi! This is my interrogation!

Robert But then again, I suspect you're like me. You don't even know the answer.

Monroe What are you, a bloody police psychologist?

Robert Dunno. I might be.

Monroe Well, I've got some bad news for you, Mr Zeinfeld. You're an accountant.

Robert An accountant?

Monroe Yep.

Robert Perfect. Thank you, God!

Monroe What's God got to do with it?

Robert I finally get the chance to experience reincarnation, and I come back as a bloody accountant.

Monroe Could be worse - you could have come back as a DI in Leicester.

Robert Or even a DC.

Monroe Oh, no, a DC would be out doing something useful, like hunting for criminals. I get stuck in here with a buffoon like you!

Robert Look, I don't like this amnesia crap any more than you do. In fact, as far as I can remember, I like it less. But I can't help it! There's nothing there. It's just like a...a black curtain, across my brain. Like some huge door has just.....you don't believe me, do you?

Monroe I'll keep an open mind.

Robert What does that mean?

Monroe It means I don't believe you.

Robert What about another bang on the head?

Monroe What?

Robert Isn't it supposed to make the memory come back sometimes?

Monroe So?

Robert Well, couldn't you just hit me on the head with a truncheon or something?

Monroe I don't think that's very scientific.

Robert It might work.

Monroe Don't get me wrong, Mr Zeinfeld. I'd love to give it a try.

Robert Well anything's better than this.

Monroe Unfortunately, I never let pleasure get in the way of my work. Besides, there's very little left to sort out. We already know who you are...

Robert Do we?

Monroe We do. So, there's just one last little detail we need to clear up, and then we can all go home.

Robert I don't want to go home.

Monroe What were you doing in Leicester?
Robert I've told you - I can't remember!
Monroe Mrs Zeinfeld says you were supposed to be in Blackpool yesterday.
Robert Does she now?
Monroe She does.
Robert Well maybe I **was** in Blackpool yesterday.
Monroe I don't think so.
Robert And what do you think?
Monroe I don't think you had time. I think you went straight to Leicester.
Robert Right then - so what does that prove?
Monroe You tell me!
Robert That Mrs Zeinfeld doesn't know what she's talking about.
Monroe Perhaps you deliberately misled Mrs Zeinfeld about going to Blackpool.
Robert Perhaps Mrs Zeinfeld deliberately misled you about me going to Blackpool.
Monroe So you still claim you can't remember why you were there?
Robert Yes.
Monroe And you can't even remember your own name.
Robert I can remember the name you said I'd got.
Monroe Robert Zeinfeld.
Robert Yes.
Monroe Is that your name?
Robert You said it was my name.
Monroe And what do you say?
Robert I say I can't remember. Why don't you ask **Mrs** Zeinfeld? She seems to have all
    the answers?
Monroe Don't worry. I have.
Robert And what does she say?
Monroe She says it's your name.
Robert Great. So we've established my name.
Monroe So you admit it is your name?
Robert What the hell, it's a good name. I'll take it!
Monroe Stop pratting about!
Robert Why are you interrogating me? I'm not a criminal, I'm a victim!
Monroe Of what?

A Flying Ducks Publication

Robert I'm found wandering around Leicester with a bump on my head. How do you know I wasn't robbed?

Monroe You weren't robbed.

Robert How do you know that?

Monroe Because nothing was missing.

Robert How do you know nothing was missing? I could have been carrying the Crown jewels.

Monroe Only if you'd stolen them.

Robert Well maybe I did, I can't remember.

Monroe You had keys, filofax, phone - there was money and credit cards in your wallet - nothing was missing.

Robert My memory was missing.

Monroe So what are you saying now - that someone bashed you over the back of the head and stole your memory?

Robert Who knows?

Monroe launches a rapid-fire onslaught.

Monroe How old are you?

Robert I can't remember!

Monroe What were you doing in Leicester?

Robert I don't know.

Monroe Where do you work?

Robert I've told you I can't...

Monroe What colour is your front door?

Robert Red!

Monroe *(a pause - slightly startled)* Was that a guess?

Robert Course it was a bloody guess! I don't even know where I live. *(Thoughtful pause)* Was it a good guess?

Monroe Not bad.

Robert What colour is it?

Monroe Green.

Robert Then it was a lousy guess.

Monroe I need a pee.

A Flying Ducks Publication

Robert How do you know?

Monroe Because my bladder is all distended.

Robert How do you know my front door is green.

Monroe I used to live there.

Robert In my house?

Monroe In Surrey. I need to go and talk to your wife.

Robert Remember me to her, would you?

Monroe goes to the door, stops and turns.

Monroe Would you like me to bring you back a coffee?

Robert Yeah, why not.

Monroe Do you take sugar?

Robert No.

Monroe *(pouncing)* Hah! How do you know that?

Robert Oh, God. That was a pathetic attempt to trick me, wasn't it?

Monroe Not so pathetic. It worked.

Robert Look, I don't know how I know. I just know, that's all. I also know that the Battle of Hastings was in 1066. Some things stick, some don't. That's just the way it is. Have you ever had amnesia?

Monroe Not as far as I can remember.

Monroe exits, and the lights fade on that side of the stage.

He enters on the other side, where Julia is waiting. He is carrying a couple of plastic cups of coffee.

Monroe Brought you a coffee.

Julia Thanks.

Monroe Couldn't remember how you said you liked it.

Julia I didn't.

Monroe Doesn't really matter. Whichever button you press it comes out undrinkable.

Julia Thanks.

Monroe You all right?

Julia I'll be okay.
Monroe You're shaking.
Julia I'll be okay!
Monroe I've just had another go at him. He still denies knowing you.
Julia I'm not surprised. That's not my husband.

Monroe, having just taken a sip of his coffee, sprays it out and drops the cup in his lap, causing momentary chaos.

Monroe What did you say?
Julia That man is not my husband.
Monroe Are you sure?
Julia Course I'm bloody sure!
Monroe Why the hell didn't you say something when you saw him?
Julia You asked me to keep my mouth shut!
Monroe Bloody hell!
Julia He looks like Robert...
Monroe Oh, that's useful!
Julia He does look...quite a lot like Robert...
Monroe Good start.
Julia But it's not him!
Monroe Then who the hell is he?
Julia You tell me.
Monroe Christ. *(He dives for the phone and starts dialling)* A man turns up at four o'clock
    in the morning...
Julia In Leicester...
Monroe With your husband's filofax...
Julia His keys...
Monroe His mobile phone...
Julia And wearing his clothes...

Monroe drops the handset into the waste paper bin in shock.

Monroe Those were his clothes??

A Flying Ducks Publication

Julia Looked damn like them to me.

Monroe Bloody hell!

Julia Look, inspector. My husband was on the eight-fifteen to Blackpool two days ago. I put him on that train myself.

Monroe Then, a man who looks like him...

Julia And wearing his things...

Monroe Turns up at Leicester at four o'clock in the morning...

Julia Claiming to have no memory.

Monroe Shit!

Julia What are we going to do?

Monroe I don't wish to be alarmist, Mrs Zeinfeld, but we could be looking at some kind of bizarre kidnapping here.

Julia Kidnapping?

Monroe Or even murder.

Julia I'd hate to meet you when you do wish to be alarmist.

Monroe Where was your husband supposed to be?

Julia Er...at a conference. Some hotel or other...

Monroe Which one?

Julia The Imperial, I think.

Monroe This is important!

Julia Yes, the Imperial.

Monroe I'll get it checked out.

Monroe makes urgently for the door.

Julia Inspector! What am I supposed to do?

Monroe Sit tight. I'm going to have another crack at that bastard.

Lights cross fade to where Robert sits, deep in thought. Monroe enters, stalking around the room for a while before speaking.

Monroe *(offering a cigarette)* Smoke?

Robert I can't remember.

Monroe Mr Zeinfeld, we have a bit of a problem here.

Robert Tell me about it.

Monroe The woman you met next door...

Robert My wife.

Monroe Your wife. Your wife now informs me...that you are not her husband.

Robert Aha. And she should know, after all she is my wife.

Monroe Apparently not.

Robert I see.

Monroe That makes things rather awkward for you, doesn't it?

Robert Awkward for me? Awkward for me? How does that make things awkward for me? I'm in Leicester, while some woman I've never seen before in my life says that her husband should be in Blackpool. Just how does that make things awkward for me?

Monroe All right then, it makes things awkward for me. Because if you're not her husband, it leaves me wondering who the hell you are. And where the bloody hell he is. Because one thing's for sure. You are certainly wearing her husband's clothes!

Robert Don't be ridiculous.

Monroe It's a fact.

Robert Who told you that - my ex-wife?

Monroe Don't get too cocky, sunshine. You're looking at very serious charges here.

Robert What charges?

Monroe How does kidnapping sound for starters?

Robert Kidnapping who?

Monroe Robert Zeinfeld.

Robert You said I was Robert Zeinfeld!

Monroe No I didn't.

Robert Excuse me! "No doubt over your identity", you said. "You are Mr Robert Zeinfeld", you said, "and that woman in there", you said, "like her or hate her, is your extremely rich wife!"

Monroe That's before I knew the full facts.

Robert What facts?

Monroe The fact that she doesn't recognize you.

Robert You said she'd identified me!

Monroe Well she hadn't actually identified you. She'd just failed to point out that she didn't identify you.

Robert You said she'd described me on the phone.

A Flying Ducks Publication

Monroe No, she'd described someone who looks like you.

Robert I look like me.

Monroe Not as much as her husband does apparently. Anyway, the fact remains, you are wearing another man's clothes.

Robert These are my clothes!

Monroe How do you know?

Robert What?

Monroe How do you know? You claim you've lost your memory.

Robert I have lost my memory.

Monroe So you can't remember whose clothes they are.

Robert I don't have to remember. Any idiot can see these are my clothes.

Monroe I can't.

Robert All right, most idiots.

Monroe Watch it!

Robert They fit me perfectly!

Monroe Only because you're the same size.

Robert The same size as who?

Monroe Robert Zeinfeld!

Robert Well that's worth knowing. Perhaps we can swap cocktail dresses sometime.

Monroe I'm due a bit of holiday this week.

Robert I'm very pleased for you.

Monroe I'm not going to take it.

Robert Why?

Monroe Because I'm going to get to the bottom of this, if it takes every last breath in my body.

Robert Well, if there's anything I can do to help...

Monroe All right, enough of the fun and games, this is getting very, very serious. Where is Robert Zeinfeld?

Robert I am Robert Zeinfeld!

Monroe How do you know?

Robert Instinct!

Monroe Bullshit!

Robert Am I under arrest?

Monroe You're under suspicion.

A Flying Ducks Publication

Robert You have to charge me or let me go.

Monroe Who says?

Robert Your colleague out there.

Monroe Oh, George. Yes, well, I have trouble with George. George has been here a thousand years and knows everything. George is the one who thinks he should have got my job. Well I've got some bad news for both of you. *(Opening the door and shouting through it to George)* He didn't get it!

Robert I want to see my lawyer.

Monroe Fine. Who is he?

Robert I can't remember.

Monroe Do you want to change your story?

Robert No. I want to adopt her story - the first one. I quite like the idea of being Mr Zeinfeld. After all, if the shoe fits...

Monroe Look, sunshine...

In the next sequence, both men are talking simultaneously. The idea is to create as much confused babble as possible, until the phone eventually interrupts them.

Robert *(spoken simultaneously with Monroe's next lines)* I can't believe you're treating me like this! Here I am - probably the victim of some horrendous mugging and all you can do...you should be out looking for the people who did this to me. Do you hear me? Look at my head! I should be in hospital.

Monroe *(spoken simultaneously with Robert's previous lines)* I've had just about enough of your smart-arse answers, so from now on, we're going to start playing this game my way. Either you tell me what the hell you've done to Robert Zeinfeld, and what the hell you were doing in Leicester, or I'm going to bang you up so fast your feet won't even...*(the phone goes)*....Monroe!! Yes, George. Right.

There's a pause, and then both men instantly start talking together again.

Robert *(spoken simultaneously with Monroe's next lines)* You can't treat me like this! I haven't done anything wrong. If you don't let me out of here I'm going to kick up such a stink you...

Monroe *(spoken simultaneously with Robert's previous lines)* Right my friend - that really puts the cat amongst the pigeons, you are officially in deep shit, pal...Shut up! *(There's a long, shocked silence, and then we revert back to normal dialogue)* Robert Zeinfeld never checked in to the hotel in Blackpool.

Robert What does that prove?

Monroe *(hesitating)* That proves that Robert Zeinfeld...

Robert Never checked in to the hotel in Blackpool.

Monroe Shut up. It proves...

Robert Absolutely nothing.

Monroe Shut up and let me think! It proves that...whatever you did to him, you did to him before he got to Blackpool.

Robert Maybe it proves that I'm Robert Zeinfeld, and that instead of going to Blackpool, I decided to go to Leicester.

Monroe Why?

Robert Perhaps I just thought that Blackpool was tacky.

Monroe So you went to Leicester.

Robert Good point. All right, perhaps I had a little business in Leicester.

Monroe What business?

Robert Can't remember.

Monroe Robert Zeinfeld had a little business in Blackpool.

Robert So did my aunt Marjorie.

Monroe What?

Robert She had a guest house on the front.

Monroe So you can't remember your name, but you can remember that you have an aunt Marjorie.

Robert No, I just made her up.

Monroe What the hell for?

Robert A bit of light relief.

Monroe What else have you been making up?

Robert What else have you got?

Another rapid exchange.

Monroe What were you doing in Leicester?

Robert I can't remember.

Monroe How old are you?

Robert I can't remember.

Monroe Who's Bobby Charlton?

Robert He was a footballer. Don't tell me he's mixed up in all of this?

Monroe Okay, that's it.

Robert That's what?

Monroe I've been here since six o'clock this morning. I'm tired. I'm fed up. I'm going to go home and get extremely drunk.

Robert What about me?

Monroe You're not invited. *(He opens the door and shouts out)* George - show the Mr Zeinfeld look-alike to his room, would you?

Robert You can't do this to me.

Monroe Yes I can. I'm a policeman.

Robert I've got my rights.

Monroe Yes, but I bet you can't remember what they are, can you?

Robert I'll write to the Home Secretary.

Monroe And who's that then, eh?

Robert Bastard.

Monroe George!

Robert is ushered to the door, but stops.

Robert Wait! This is ridiculous.

Monroe Ridiculous, is it?

Robert Well, I mean the whole thing's just so easy to prove.

Monroe Oh, terrific! Well, I'll go home and get drunk, you stay here and wrap up the case for me.

Robert That picture you took of me last night.

Monroe What about it?

Robert Why don't you just show it to her neighbours, and ask them who I am?

Monroe Huh! Don't you think I haven't thought of that? *(A quick thought flashes across his eyes, which suggest he hadn't thought of it. He shouts to George)* Lock him up!

Robert exits. Monroe makes straight for the phone.

A Flying Ducks Publication

Monroe George? The mug shot you took of our mutual friend. Fax it over to the Surrey mob, will you? Ask them to show it to Mrs Zeinfeld's neighbours. I just want to know if they recognize him. Yes, well I know you're terribly busy at the moment, George. But I thought you could squeeze it in immediately after locking up our friend and immediately before going back to playing Patience on the computer. Yeah, well if you want to shove a broom up your arse as well that's fine by me. Oh - any luck with the phone charger? Oh, right, good. No, no, no - it's all right, George, I'll come in and get it. I don't want you triple-tasking. *(He puts the phone down)*

The inspector exits, and re-appears in the other room with the phone charger. He plugs the phone in and fiddles with it as he's talking.

Julia About bloody time! What the hell's going on?

Monroe I've locked him away for the night.

Julia What's he saying in there?

Monroe Not much. But he'll crack, sooner or later. Are you sure you don't know this pin number?

Julia Positive. Look, how long's all this going to take?

Monroe Well, let me see now. Interrogation, confession, collating evidence, presenting to the Crown Prosecution Service, trial, appeal...about seventeen years should cover it.

Julia I want to go home.

Monroe That makes two of us. *(Handing her a card)* If you think of anything urgent - that's my direct number. But don't bother ringing it, I'll be at home. Either way, I need to see you back here tomorrow.

Julia You are joking?

Monroe Notorious for it. All the lads call me Oscar Wilde.

Julia I'm sorry. I'm not coming back. I've got urgent business.

Monroe And I've got urgent questions.

Julia Then you'll have to ring me.

She makes for the door, and is stopped by Monroe.

Monroe Mrs Zeinfeld. Do you have a photograph of your husband?

Julia A photograph?
Monroe It's like a drawing, only better.
Julia My God, you **are** Oscar Wilde.
Monroe Have you got one?
Julia No.
Monroe No?
Julia Well, not on me.
Monroe But you do have one?
Julia Probably. At home. Why?
Monroe If we're going to start searching for your husband, it helps to know what he looks
    like.
Julia Oh, right. I'll post you one. *(Again she goes to leave)*
Monroe Mrs Zeinfeld...
Julia What?
Monroe First class stamp.

She exits, hurriedly.

Monroe *(sarcastically)* Thanks for coming.

He has another fruitless few goes at the phone, and we again hear the amplified results.

Finally, in frustration, Monroe smacks the phone on the desk four times. To his amazement, it then continues:

"You have one new message. Main menu options. To listen to your messages, press one..."

He presses the key eagerly.

"First new message. Message received yesterday at 8.51pm..."

We then hear the voice of a female.

"It's me. We need to talk. Ring me."

Monroe Got you!

This is followed once again by the answerphone announcer:

To listen to the message again, press one. To save the message, press two, to delete the message, press three".

Monroe presses one and hears the message again, this time recording it on his memo machine. He plays it back to himself a few times.

Monroe Right, young lady - who the hell are you?

The lights cut to black, and we hear the answerphone message: "You have reached the mailbox of Robert Zeinfeld. Please speak after the tone."

Lights cut to a spotlight on Samantha, on a mobile phone.

Samantha Why are you ignoring me? Look, don't push it, Robert. We need to talk. I'm warning you, if you don't ring me back by tomorrow, I'll phone you at home. Ball's in your court, darling."

The spotlight fades on Samantha. It is the next morning. The phone in Monroe's office is ringing. He eventually enters, carrying a plastic cup of coffee, and answers it.

Monroe Monroe? Yes, George. Well I was getting myself a cup of coffee, it that's all right with you, George. What's she doing here? All right, send her in.

Mrs Zeinfeld enters. Her general attitude is less aggressive than that of the previous day.

Monroe Mrs Zeinfeld. I trust we reserved your usual parking space?
Julia You asked for a photograph. I thought it might speed things up if I brought it myself.
Monroe I thought you had urgent business.
Julia I cancelled it.

A Flying Ducks Publication

Monroe Very helpful. *(He takes a sip of his coffee)* Can I get you one?
Julia No, thanks.
Monroe Let's have a butcher's, then.
Julia Any news?
Monroe Not really. Weird character. Still claims to have no memory at all. He totally denied being Robert Zeinfeld, right up to the point when I told him that he wasn't Robert Zeinfeld. Now he's suddenly decided he wants to be Robert Zeinfeld.
Julia That's because he is.

Monroe again drops the coffee on his trousers.

Monroe What?
Julia He is my husband.
Monroe Who is?
Julia The man in there.
Monroe You're joking?
Julia Just call me Oscar Wilde.
Monroe You're not joking.
Julia No.
Monroe You're trying to tell me that...two days I've been grinding that bugger down! First I tell him he's Robert Zeinfeld, then I have to tell him he's not Robert Zeinfeld...now you're asking me to go in there and tell him he's Robert bloody Zeinfeld?
Julia I'm not asking you to do anything. I'm just telling you the facts.
Monroe What facts? Yesterday's facts or today's facts?
Julia I don't like it any more than you do, inspector. But he is Robert Zeinfeld.

A pause, while Monroe simmers.

Monroe Look at my bloody trousers!
Julia I'll buy you a new suit.
Monroe I don't need a new suit!
Julia Trust me. You need a new suit.

Another long, simmering pause.

A Flying Ducks Publication

Monroe Well this changes things.

Julia I suppose it does.

Monroe This definitely changes things.

Julia Yes.

Monroe So, let me get this straight. You're definitely changing your story.

Julia Do you believe me?

Monroe Do I believe you're changing your story?

Julia Do you believe I'm telling the truth?

Monroe When? Then? Or now?

Julia Do you believe I was telling you the truth when I said I was lying?

Monroe I don't even understand the question.

Julia Here. The camera never lies, so they say. *(She passes him a photograph from her handbag)*

Monroe This is you. And him!

Julia Yes. We were younger then, of course, and happier.

Monroe When was this taken?

Julia Last Wednesday.

Monroe *(suddenly exploding)* So why did you say it wasn't him!

Julia Well, we don't exactly get along and, well, it occurred to me that this might be a good excuse to, well, get rid of him.

Monroe Get rid of him?!

Julia It's a long story.

Monroe I'm not going anywhere.

While Mrs Zeinfeld explains, Monroe decides to try and dry his crutch, crouching awkwardly in front of an office desk fan.

Julia As I said, Robert was the company's accountant. Bit of a boring bastard really.

Monroe Why did you marry him?

Julia He had a nice bottom.

Monroe A nice bottom.

Julia Yes. Unfortunately the line of his bottom turned out to be in somewhat better shape than his bottom line, if you follow me.

Monroe I'm trying.

Julia Daddy sacked him. Robert went to work for a rival firm, and a bit of a feud developed between them.

Monroe Whose side were you on?

Julia Don't be ridiculous. My father is one of the richest men in Britain.

Monroe Carry on.

Julia Well, a divorce was pending - it was all going to get very costly. Then this amnesia business came up. It struck me as a neat way of cutting the divorce bill, and teaching him a lesson.

Monroe For what?

Julia For messing around with that little tart of his.

Monroe What tart?

Julia Well, I don't know all that much about her really. But I think you'll find she lives in Leicester.

Monroe Ah. *(He passes her the memo machine recording of the phone call to listen to)* Do you recognize that voice?

Julia No. Who is she?

Monroe Dunno. Not local though I don't think. Sounds more like from down your way. She could hold the key to what happened.

Julia Chances are, they had a row the other night - she smashes him over the head with a frying pan, and sends him off onto the streets. Sorry to disappoint you, inspector, but what I think you have here is a rather messy little domestic. Not really a police matter at all.

Monroe It never occurred to you he might get his memory back?

Julia It was just an opportunist thing. I hadn't really thought it through.

Monroe That's today's understatement!

Julia Look, when a police inspector asks you if someone is your husband, you tend to have to say yes or no. It's hard to play for time. I just grabbed at it. Then, when you started to talk about murder and photographs and all the rest of it, I started to panic. It was just a stupid joke.

Monroe So he hasn't stolen your husband's clothes.

Julia No.

Monroe Or his filofax.

Julia No.

Monroe And he hasn't really lost his memory.

Julia I doubt it. That's probably the first thing he could think of when he was picked up.

Monroe I could do you for wasting police time.

Julia I know.

Monroe But that would only result in wasting more police time, and I've got some holiday coming. Get out.

Julia There was something else I meant to mention. This mystery woman, the tart on the phone. If you do track her down, you will let me know, won't you?

Monroe And why should I do that?

Julia Well, let's put it this way. Robert and I will be having a divorce. And if my lawyers can prove adultery, that divorce will be an awful lot cheaper.

Monroe So I'd be doing you a big favour.

Julia Yes.

Monroe And dropping your husband in the shit.

Julia Exactly.

Monroe And why should I help out a woman who's just wasted two days of my time.

Julia Because if I can I save a lot of money, I don't mind sharing a little of it. With my friends.

Monroe What are you trying to say?

Julia Just a name and an address. Scribbled on a bit of paper. Five thousand pounds?

Monroe swallows hard.

Monroe I think you need to hire yourself a grubby little private detective, Mrs Zeinfeld.

Julia I thought I just had. Think it over, inspector. Name and address - that's all I want. Nothing illegal in that, is there? Anyway, you've got my number.

She exits.

Monroe Bloody cheek!

The lights cross fade, as Monroe enters to address Robert.

Monroe All right, Mr Zeinfeld. Off you go.

A Flying Ducks Publication

Robert I'm free to go?

Monroe Yep.

Robert Why?

Monroe Because you're Robert Zeinfeld.

Robert I am?

Monroe You are.

Robert But you said I wasn't.

Monroe No I didn't.

Robert Oh, come on! What are you trying to do here? Freak me out?

Monroe I said you **were** Robert Zeinfeld.

Robert That was the first time. The second time you...

Monroe I never actually said that you weren't Robert Zeinfeld.

Robert You said I'd kidnapped him!

Monroe I merely asked the question.

Robert You said I was wearing his clothes.

Monroe You **are** wearing his clothes.

Robert Another man's clothes - that's what you said.

Monroe You know, for someone with a dodgy memory you don't miss much, do you?

Robert Are you taping these interviews?

Monroe Might be.

Robert Right, play me back the bit where you said...

Monroe All right, all right! So the second time I might have implied that you weren't Robert Zeinfeld.

Robert Stated.

Monroe Implied.

Robert Stated!

Monroe Stated by implication.

Robert Stated by statement.

Monroe You're beginning to annoy me.

Robert Only just? You've been annoying me for two days.

Monroe Well I'm very sorry!

Robert So you should be! It's not a very nice feeling, you know, having no memory. No past. Nothing to hang on to. Jesus, talk about an identity crisis. Right now I just want to be somebody, you know? I just want to be the same person for more than ten minutes in a row. And all you do is keep coming in here and confusing the hell out of me.

Monroe I had my reasons.

Robert What reasons?

Monroe I don't want to talk about it.

Robert Now just hang on a minute! This is my life you're playing with here!

Monroe All right - I said you weren't, because she said you weren't.

Robert And now she says I am?

Monroe Woman's prerogative.

Robert She's changed her mind again?

Monroe Yes. It appears she was initially telling me the truth, but under intensive scrutiny she finally broke down and lied to me.

Robert What?

Monroe No, I don't understand it either.

Robert This is outrageous. I'm not having this.

Monroe What do you mean, you're not having it? You've got no choice.

Robert I refuse to be pigeon-holed like this, like some bloody....pigeon...in a hole.

Monroe You are who you are.

Robert No! I am not who I am!

Monroe Look, I've seen proof - trust me.

Robert What proof?

Monroe A photograph.

Robert What photograph?

Monroe Of the two of you together.

Robert Me and Robert Zeinfeld?

Monroe You and Mrs Zeinfeld.

Robert Photographs can be faked.

Monroe For God's sake man! Stop fighting it! Yesterday you wanted to **be** Robert Zeinfeld!

Robert Yes. And you wouldn't let me!

Monroe Well now I'm letting you!

Robert Well, now I'm not so sure.

Monroe You contrary bastard!

Robert *Me* contrary? What about you? What about her!

Monroe Here's Mr Zeinfeld's filofax. Mr Zeinfeld's briefcase. Mr Zeinfeld's keys. You're wearing Mr Zeinfeld's clothes. Get out, and get on with it!

Robert makes for the door, stops and turns.

Robert Why the hell would she say I wasn't if I was?
Monroe To teach you a lesson.
Robert What for?
Monroe Apparently, you were having an affair.
Robert Was I?
Monroe Yes.
Robert Who with?
Monroe We don't know.
Robert What - none of us?
Monroe No.
Robert Terrific.
Monroe If I find out I'll let you know.
Robert Thanks.
Monroe Don't mention it. *(An awkward silence)* Right. Well. *(He offers a handshake)* It's been nice not knowing you.
Robert You're just saying that.
Monroe No, really. You're just about the most interesting thing that's happened to me since I came to Leicester.
Robert That's a real accolade.

Another awkward pause.

Monroe Well?
Robert Well what?
Monroe Bugger off.

Robert slowly opens the door, but is stopped by Monroe.

Monroe Just a minute. Was it a frying pan?

A Flying Ducks Publication

Robert Was what a frying pan?
Monroe Never mind. Have nice life.
Robert Have a good holiday.

Robert again goes to exit, but then he lingers, bewildered, like a lost child.

Monroe What's up?
Robert I don't want to go.
Monroe Don't be stupid.
Robert I don't even know where I'm going.
Monroe The address is in the filofax.
Robert I don't want to go there!
Monroe It's a very nice house - trust me.
Robert I don't even know who I am!
Monroe You're Robert Zeinfeld.
Robert You're asking me to go back to a woman I don't even know.
Monroe That's not my problem.
Robert Can't I stay here?
Monroe No!
Robert Just for a couple of days, till I get myself sorted out.
Monroe This is a police station, not a bloody hotel!
Robert I'll sleep in the cells.
Monroe No!
Robert I won't be any trouble.
Monroe No!!
Robert Please!
Monroe No!!!
Robert Just one damp cell for the night!
Monroe You can't!
Robert Why not?
Monroe You're not under arrest!

Robert knees Monroe in the groin. He immediately collapses.

Monroe You're under arrest.
Robert Thanks. Don't get up. I know the way.

Robert exits. Monroe crawls to the phone and drags it down onto his lap. He punches in George's number and mutters to himself.

Monroe If you don't answer this phone, George, I swear you'll be a dustbin man by Monday morning. Ah, George, my trusty soldier, now listen carefully. Mr Zeinfeld is on his way out to you. I want you to put him up for the night - all expenses paid. Yes. That's right, he's under arrest. Assaulting a police officer. Look, he just assaulted me, that's all you need to know. George, just put...just lock the bugger up, would you? That's all you need to know. Look, forget the bloody paperwork for once in your life, George....I know it's unorthodox, but the...look! He kneed me in the bollocks, all right? George....George! Yes, ha bloody ha! Me and you are going to fall out, George - big time!

He slams the phone down, lifts himself up and dusts himself down - checking all vital equipment is still intact. He grabs an overcoat, turns out the light and is halfway out of the door when the phone rings again. He considers ignoring it, but finally gives in. The main light stays off, Monroe switching on just a desk lamp to take the call.

Monroe? Oh, hello Frank - long time no speak. How are things down in leafy Surrey, then? Oh, I'm all right. Still trying to find my feet, you know. And to what do I owe this honour? Oh, yes. Oh, right, and you got the short straw did you? Yeah. Right. What? Say that again. You're having me on. Bloody hell! Thanks, Frank. *(He urgently slams down the phone and picks it back up for an internal call)* George - have you locked Zeinfeld up yet? Well get him out! Oh, nothing much. I've just had the Surrey mob on. Remember the picture you faxed over? They showed it to Mrs Zeinfeld's neighbours. They've never seen him before in their lives. Whoever that man is, he is not Robert Zeinfeld!

Lights to black. End of Act One.

ACT TWO

Monroe All right. Let's start again shall we? I am tired, and my balls are aching.
Robert I've said I'm sorry.
Monroe Oh, that's a big help.
Robert What do you want me to do? Kiss it better?
Monroe I'll stick with the apology.
Robert It was just a knee-jerk reaction.
Monroe Now, listen very carefully. I want you to cast your mind, or what's left of it, back half an hour or so. Do you recall, moments before you brought your right knee sharply up into my gonads, that you expressed grave doubts about being one Robert Zeinfeld?
Robert Yes.
Monroe Do you still hold those doubts?
Robert Do you still hold those gonads?
Monroe Don't push it, I'm not in the mood.
Robert Sorry.
Monroe Do you still hold those doubts?
Robert Yes.
Monroe Will you still hold those doubts, regardless of what I am about to say?
Robert That depends.
Monroe On what?
Robert On what you are about to say.
Monroe All right then, let me say it. I now have incontrovertible proof that you are not Robert Zeinfeld.
Robert Incontrovertible proof.
Monroe Yes.
Robert Is this anything like the incontrovertible proof you had that I **was** Robert Zeinfeld?
Monroe Better.
Robert Better than the photograph?
Monroe Photographs can be faked.
Robert That was my line.
Monroe Well, now I'm agreeing with you.
Robert That worries me.

A Flying Ducks Publication

Monroe And don't even bother asking me what the proof is.

Robert What's the proof?

Monroe I'm not telling you.

Robert Why not?

Monroe It's classified.

Robert Very impressive. What does that mean?

Monroe It means I'm not telling you. In fact, from now on, everything I tell you is on a strictly need-to-know basis.

Robert Good. I need to know.

Monroe Not yet you don't.

Robert When then?

Monroe When I'm good and ready.

Robert Leaving aside the thorny question of whether you'll ever be good - will you ever be ready?

Monroe As it happens, I think I've finally started to make some real progress with this case.

Robert Such as?

Monroe That would be telling.

Robert In other words, you know bugger all.

Closing in on Robert, eyeball to eyeball.

Monroe I know more than you think I know.

Robert That depends how much I think you know.

Monroe reflects on this momentarily, and then backs off, confused.

Monroe All right then, try to follow my logic here. Ready?

Robert Hanging on to your every word.

Monroe Right. Fact number one. I don't know, whether you really know, who you are or not. Right?

Robert Meaning what?

Monroe Meaning, maybe you've lost your memory - maybe you haven't. The fact is, I don't know.

Robert You're right, that does sound like real progress.

A Flying Ducks Publication

Monroe Shut up - I haven't finished yet. Now, let's just say, for the moment, that I've given you the benefit of the doubt.

Robert Thanks. I knew that knee in the bollocks would soften you up.

Monroe Fact number two. You are not Robert Zeinfeld.

Robert At least for the next twenty minutes or so.

Monroe Fact number three. If you are **not** Mr Zeinfeld - and I now have incontrovertible proof that you are not - then **Mrs** Zeinfeld must **know** that you are not Mr Zeinfeld. Correct?

Robert A fair assumption. Most wives tend to be able to recognize their husbands.

Monroe Fact number four. Mrs Zeinfeld said that you **were** Mr Zeinfeld. So, two possible conclusions. A: Mrs Zeinfeld is really Mrs Magoo, and foolishly forgot to bring her spectacles to the station. Or B: - and this is the theory I favour - Mrs Zeinfeld is telling porkies.

Robert *(in mock awe)* Amazing! So you've now deduced that a woman who's already changed her story three times might just possibly be a liar. I tell you what, inspector, Sherlock Holmes would have been proud.

Monroe You know, there's an old saying in the force. A policeman with bruised nuts, is a dangerous policeman.

Robert I'll try and remember that. Okay. So we know that Mrs Zeinfeld's lying. Why don't you arrest her?

Monroe I'm on to that.

Robert What do you mean, you're on to it?

Monroe I'm having her front door watched.

Robert The green one.

Monroe Yes, the green one.

Robert Look, I'm no expert in police tactics, inspector, but instead of watching her front door, why don't you go up to it, knock on it, wait for it to open, and then extract her through it?

Monroe Because, smartarse, Mrs Zeinfeld is not currently behind it. She appears to have disappeared.

Robert She appears to have disappeared?

Monroe All right then, she has disappeared! What is this - a bloody English lesson?

Robert Just because your balls ache, there's no need to become ungrammatical.

Monroe Who do you think you're talking to?

Robert To whom do I think I'm talking.

Monroe There's some serious hanky panky going on here. To which...the bottom of...I intend to get. Now, you are going to spend the rest of the night in the cells. But I just wanted you to know that you are no longer there because you want to be there. You are now there because I want you to be there. Goodnight.

Robert So, just for the record, inspector, before I retire for the evening with a mug of Her Majesty's cocoa, let me get one thing straight. I am no longer to think of myself as Robert Zeinfeld - is that the latest theory?

Monroe You are not Robert Zeinfeld.

Robert And we're sure about this.

Monroe We have proof.

Robert Incontrovertible.

Monroe Yes. Goodnight.

Robert Write it down.

Monroe What?

Robert Can you write it down please.

Monroe Don't be ridiculous.

Robert I see.

Monroe What do you mean, you see? You see what? What do you see?

Robert Nothing.

Monroe Come on. Spit it out.

Robert There's nothing to spit out.

Monroe Oh, no. You're not getting away with that. You can't go around saying "I see" in that smarmy bloody know-all way of yours without telling me what it is you think you see. Come on, out with it.

Robert All right. It's quite obvious that you're going to change your mind again.

Monroe I am not going to change my mind!

Robert Yes you are.

Monroe No I'm not!

Robert I bet you'll stroll in here tomorrow morning, bright and breezy, say "Oh, by the way, did I mention, you are Robert Zeinfeld after all", and then deny you ever said any different.

Monroe No I won't!

Robert Then what's the problem? Just write it down. "You are not Robert Zeinfeld."

Forget-Me-Knot

Simple statement. That's all I want. A little security in a crazy world.

Monroe All right. *(He tetchily grabs a piece of paper and hastily scribbles the note)* Satisfied?

Robert Sign it. *(Monroe glares, then signs)* Time and date. *(Monroe again obliges. Robert checks the paper, folds it carefully and puts it in his shirt pocket)* Thank you.

Monroe Don't mention it.

Robert Let's hope I don't have to.

Monroe sees Robert out through the door with a final glare and a short word to George.

Monroe George!

The lights black out. We hear Robert Zeinfeld's answerphone message - a female voice. "I'm sorry, Robert can't come to the phone right now. If you'd like to leave your name and number, he'll get back to you." The lights cut to a spotlight on Samantha, making the call.

Samantha This is not funny, Robert. I rang your home tonight and guess what? Little wifey answered. Next time I swear I'm going to have a nice little chat with her. All right, look. I'm sorry about the frying pan. Okay? Now, can we all turn back into adults and talk to each other? I'll give you one last chance. If you don't...*(we hear the sound of a door shutting)*...saved by the door. Hubby's back. I'll call you tomorrow, and you'd better have some smart answers, or else the sh.....

The door opens, and she hastily ends the call. In walks Inspector Monroe.

Samantha Had a good day?

Monroe Oh, just the usual. First I find a man who says he doesn't know who he is. Then I meet a woman who says she's his wife. Then she isn't. Then she is. Then she tries to bribe me to find his girlfriend. Then he knees me in the nuts because he wants to stay in gaol. Pretty average stuff, really.

Samantha *(not listening)* Good, okay, well I'm going to have to go to work. There's some of that paella crap in the microwave. See you later.

She exits hurriedly.

A Flying Ducks Publication

Monroe Thanks for listening.

She enters again, frantically hunting for something.

Monroe What have you lost?
Samantha Keys.
Monroe Where did you put them?
Samantha If I could remember where I'd put them I wouldn't have lost them, would I?
   Shift your bum.

She delves around the chair he's sitting on, unsuccessfully.

Monroe Ever come across anybody with amnesia?
Samantha Amnesia?
Monroe Loss of memory.
Samantha I know what bloody amnesia means.
Monroe Interesting stuff.
Samantha Look, I've just lost my keys - it doesn't mean I've got senile dementia.
Monroe No, it's just a case I'm working on at the moment. Some bloke reckons he's got
   amnesia.
Samantha What are the symptoms?
Monroe He can't remember anything.
Samantha Get away.
Monroe No, I mean anything - his name, where he lives - the works.
Samantha Has he had a bang on the head?
Monroe Yeah, but nothing that looks too serious.
Samantha Where the bloody hell have I put them?
Monroe Haven't got any spare time tomorrow, have you?
Samantha I doubt it. Why?
Monroe Just wondered if you could pop in - have look at him. See if he's for real or just
   acting.
Samantha I'm a doctor, not a drama adjudicator. Hasn't he seen anybody?

A Flying Ducks Publication

She pops out of the door, still searching.

Monroe *(shouting to her outside the door)* Yeah, well, old Potter had a quick look at him, but you know Potter - if it doesn't involve antibiotics he's stumped. I'd value a second opinion.
Samantha Got them!
Monroe Where were they?
Samantha *(popping her head round the door)* In the microwave.
Monroe Try and pop in tomorrow.
Samantha I've got to go.

She dashes out.

Monroe Nice to see you.

The lights black out. As they fade back up, we can hear the internal phone ringing in the background. Monroe enters his office, carrying a large cardboard box, stamped "Property of Police Stores", which he places on the desk. He momentarily checks that his phone, which is off the hook, is still ringing out, and then opens the box. He get a megaphone out of it, then opens the door and uses it to address those outside.

Monroe "This is the Police! Move away from the computer. You are surrounded by phones. Pick up the one that's making a noise, you useless, lazy, deaf bastards!" *(The ringing finally stops)* Thank you. *(He returns to the phone)* George? Derek - where's George? Dentist's again? That man must have more teeth than a fucking shark. This wouldn't have anything to do with the fact that it's Friday again, would it? When's he back? Three o'clock? What's he doing, having his head filled? All right, Derek, listen...hang on. Dentist's - there's a thought. How do we stand on having somebody identified through their dental records? I'm thinking about this Zeinfeld character. I dunno. I presume we'd have to get him to bite on a plasticine sandwich or something. Look into it, would you? Thanks, Derek.

Monroe puts down the phone and stares thoughtfully for a second. Then he picks up the phone again.

Monroe Derek. I've just remembered why I phoned you. Any news on Mrs Zeinfeld yet? Oh, is she now? Wonderful. And how angry is she? Excellent. Right, well stick a cup of coffee in her trap and sling her in my direction. I'm just in the mood for a good scrap.

Robert Zeinfeld's mobile rings. Monroe reaches out and answers it automatically, without realizing the significance of which phone it is.

Monroe Yeah?

A spotlight picks out Samantha, making the call on her mobile.

Samantha Now, this is the way I see it. We both had a tough week. You got mad at me. I got mad at you. So let's settle this like adults. You meet me outside the hospital at eight o'clock tonight. We'll go for a little Italian food, bottle of wine. Then you can drive me over to that little deserted farmyard in Edgeware Lane, wind down the front seats, tear off my clothes and take out all that pent-up frustration on my naked, writhing torso. How's that sound?
Monroe *(shocked but delighted)* Sounds okay to me, love.
Samantha Shit! Who is this?
Monroe It's me!
Samantha Right - of course it is. Right...I'll, er...I'll see you later then.

She hastily ends the call. He momentarily double-takes, unsure which phone he's answered the call on, then shakes it off. She's in a state of total panic.

Samantha You stupid cow, Samantha! If you're going to invite someone for a crafty shag at least make sure you press the right button! Christ! What am I going to do? I've just invited my own husband for a night of dirty sex!

She thinks for a second, then presses another number. Monroe's office phone rings. He answers it.

A Flying Ducks Publication

Monroe Monroe?

Samantha Me again.

Monroe The answer's still yes.

Samantha Look, would you believe it? No sooner do I put the phone down then we get a multiple pile-up on the motorway. I'm going to be stuck at the hospital for hours.

Monroe Oh, right.

Samantha I know. I was looking forward to it as well. Never mind. See you later on.

Monroe Which motorway?

Samantha Sixty-nine. *(Putting her hand over the phone)* I can't believe I just said that. Anyway, got to go. See you later.

Monroe I take it you're not going to have time to come and examine this Zeinfeld character then.

Samantha Zeinfeld?

Monroe The amnesia bloke I mentioned to you last night. You probably weren't listening.

Samantha No, I was. It's just that....Zeinfeld?

Monroe Yeah, you remember the Zeinfelds from the Wentworth estate? Well it's one of them. Except it's not one of them. It's somebody impersonating one of them. Long story. Anyway, I'd better let you get on.

Samantha Which Zeinfeld?

Monroe Robert.

Samantha Jesus Christ!

Monroe What - you know him?

Samantha Well, I think I might have come across him once or twice.

Monroe When?

Samantha Oh, from when we worked in Surrey. At the hospital. I think I might have treated him.

Monroe You wouldn't recognize him, would you?

Samantha Possibly.

Monroe Well, that should be interesting. Look, tell you what - I'll bring you a photo home tonight.

Samantha Don't bother. I'll come over now.

Monroe What about your crash victims?

Samantha Sod 'em.

A Flying Ducks Publication

She ends the call, and the lights fade on Samantha as a bawling Mrs Zeinfeld enters Monroe's office.

Julia I don't want a bloody coffee!
Monroe Mrs Zeinfeld!
Julia What the hell's going on?
Monroe Always a cheery smile.
Julia Why am I under arrest?
Monroe Because you've been naughty, and I'm a policeman.
Julia I did not try to bribe you.
Monroe Who said anything about a bribe?
Julia It was a friendly gesture, that's all - to help you buy a new suit.
Monroe Oh, you mean your sordid little proposition. No, nothing to do with that. In fact, I was quite tempted. Who wouldn't be? Five grand for a name I would have given you anyway. Better than a kick in the nuts, isn't it? And, believe me, I should know.
Julia Then why am I here?
Monroe Because you've been telling porkies, haven't you.
Julia I've already admitted I lied.
Monroe Ah, but when you admitted you lied were you telling the truth?
Julia What the hell are you talking about?
Monroe I'm talking about your husband.
Julia What about him?
Monroe You said he was your husband.
Julia He was. He is!
Monroe Ah, but he isn't, is he?
Julia What?
Monroe He's not Robert Zeinfeld. We checked.
Julia What do you mean, you checked? Who with?
Monroe We showed his picture to the neighbours. Never seen him before in their lives.
Julia *(head in hands)* Oh, shit!
Monroe Precisely. And you're the one that's in it. Right up to your... *(he twiddles one of her dangly earrings)* ...dangly bits.
Julia I can explain.

A Flying Ducks Publication

Monroe Good! Good. I'm looking forward to it. In fact, we've been having a bit of a sweepstake round the office. Where are we now? *(Finding a piece of paper)* Ah, yes, here's the latest betting. "Reasons why Mr Zeinfeld wasn't recognized by his neighbours..." 2-1 favourite... "Mr Zeinfeld doesn't get out much." Or perhaps you fancy the 10-1 shot... "Mr Zeinfeld normally wears a full beard." And what's this one? Oh yes, 11-4 second favourite... "That wasn't really the neighbours, it was just people who looked like them and were wearing their clothes."

Julia Do you want me to explain or not?

Monroe Make it a good one. I've got a tenner riding on this.

Julia They must have shown the picture to Benny.

Monroe "Must have shown the picture to Benny..." no, that's not one of the front-runners. Oh, hang on, I suppose it could come under the 4-1 shot... "Any other bollocks she makes up on the spot."

Julia Benny is the old git next door.

Monroe Right, and what? His eyes have gone, have they?

Julia The other side are away on holiday, so it must have been Benny.

Monroe You're not making any sense, Mrs Zeinfeld.

Julia Look, I rang Benny when I first had this mad idea about saying Robert wasn't Robert. I told him to deny knowing Robert if the Police ever came round with a picture.

Monroe Why?

Julia To cover my story.

Monroe And he agreed?

Julia Delighted. He hates Robert. Anything to get him into trouble, he said. It's another long story.

Monroe More of a tall one, I'd say.

Julia It all started when Robert borrowed Benny's electric hedge trimmers.

Monroe This is going to be a corker. I can feel it in my bowels. Go on.

Julia Well, Robert accidentally sliced the head off one of Benny's topiary peacocks.

Monroe *(flatly, after a pause)* Topiary peacocks.

Julia Yes. Apparently it had taken him fourteen years to grow them. He's got a row of three, you see, and he wasn't best pleased when the middle one's head suddenly, sort of...dropped off. Robert tried to stick it back on with parcel tape, but it went brown and shrivelled up and...well, it didn't look the same.

Monroe *(after a deep sigh)* You know what's so tragic about all this, Mrs Zeinfeld?

A Flying Ducks Publication

Julia What?

Monroe The fact that I believe you. You know why I believe you, don't you.

Julia Why?

Monroe *(he slowly closes in on her, eyeball to eyeball, his enunciation very slow, deliberate and threatening, before finally exploding)* Because nobody... nobody, Mrs Zeinfeld... would have the bottle to come in here, after everything you've done to me, and start fabricating stories about a topiary...fucking...pheasant! Now would they?

Julia Peacock.

Monroe What?

Julia It was a peacock, not a pheasant.

Monroe Mrs Zeinfeld, I don't care if it was an elephant's dick.

Julia You might have been trying to catch me out.

Monroe God forbid I should find a hole in your story, Mrs Zeinfeld.

Julia Just saying.

Monroe So, it was a peacock.

Julia Yes. Made out of privet hedge.

Monroe Topiary.

Julia Exactly. But with no head.

Monroe Right. So, as I was saying, either you're on some very impressive hallucinatory drug - in which case I want the name of the dealer - or you're telling the truth.

Julia I always tell the truth in the end.

Monroe Ah, but is this the end?

Julia Why don't you just phone Benny and ask him?

Monroe You mean Benny, the next-door neighbour who lies to the police? That Benny?

Julia All right, you've made your point.

Monroe I might as well ask the bloody peacocks.

Julia You wouldn't get much sense out of the middle one.

Samantha enters.

Monroe Oh, you made it!

Samantha Have to be quick.

Monroe He's in Interview One. But there's something I've got to do first. Give me a couple of ticks. I'm sure you two can find something to chat about. This is Mrs Zeinfeld.

He exits, leaving a nervous Samantha exposed to her lover's wife.

Samantha Mrs Zeinfeld. What a...a thing it is to meet you.
Julia It's a thing to meet you too, dear.

A nervous pause.

Samantha I do like those earrings.
Julia No you don't.
Samantha Can I er...get you a drink of something?
Julia No thank you.
Samantha Coffee?
Julia No thank you.
Samantha Tea?
Julia No!
Samantha Hot chocolate!

Mrs Zeinfeld finally answers with a glare.

Samantha Right, well...I'll be erm...bye, then.

Samantha darts out. The lights cross-fade to the other side, where Robert sits in silence as Monroe enters. Monroe slowly goes up to him, reaches for the piece of paper inside Robert's shirt pocket, ritualistically tears it up, and hands back the pieces to Robert, who accepts them, nodding resignedly.

Robert *(producing another piece of paper)* I had George do me a photostat.

Monroe snatches this out of his hand as well and tears it up, then goes to leave.

Robert Inspector? Just tell me why.
Monroe Topiary peacocks.
Robert Right.

A Flying Ducks Publication

Again Monroe goes to leave, but is stopped as Robert lets rips with a blood-curdling scream of frustration and bangs his head repeatedly on the table.

Monroe Feel better now?

Robert Yes, thank you.

Monroe Good.

Robert Inspector. Am I rich?

Monroe Yes.

Robert Right. Five grand says you change your mind about my identity at least once more before the day's out.

Monroe What is it about you Zeinfelds? You're all trying to thrust money at me.

Robert You say you're not going to change your mind. I'm just trying to test your conviction. Five grand's a pretty good test.

Monroe Five grand.

Robert Make it ten if you want.

Monroe You might be a rich man, Mr Zeinfeld, but I'm not.

Robert So you are going to change your mind.

Monroe No.

Robert Are you sure?

Monroe Positive.

Robert Then it doesn't matter, does it? It'll be the easiest ten grand you'll ever make.

Monroe considers carefully.

Monroe You realize that if I did change my mind, it would mean that you're not Robert Zeinfeld, so you wouldn't be rich any more.

Robert That's okay. At least I'd have your ten grand.

Monroe I haven't got ten grand.

Robert You will have, if you don't change your mind. Look, I'm not interested in the money, inspector. I just want my identity back. Come on, convince me that you're convinced.

After another thoughtful pause, Monroe shakes hands with Robert. Samantha enters.

Monroe Oh, by the way, Mr Zeinfeld. You don't mind if I call you Mr Zeinfeld, do you?
Robert I don't give a toss any more. You can call me Zebbedee as far as I'm concerned.
Monroe Right, Zebbedee. The doctor here would like to have a quick look at your head, if you don't mind.
Robert Help yourself.
Monroe You'll find it on the top of his spring.
Samantha Erm...could you get me a coffee?
Monroe Course. How do you take it?
Samantha Black, no sugar.
Monroe That's it. I did know.

Monroe exits.

Samantha Robert. Do you know who I am?
Robert Yes.
Samantha Who am I?
Robert You're a doctor.
Samantha Is that all?
Robert What else do you want to be?
Samantha Bloody hell, you have lost your memory. Well, let's see if this helps.

She gives him a passionate kiss, breaking off just as Monroe re-enters with the coffee.

Monroe Well, what do you reckon?
Robert She's magnificent.
Monroe I wasn't talking to you.
Samantha I'd like to do some more tests.
Monroe Any objection if the doctor does some more tests on you?
Robert None whatsoever.
Monroe *(to Samantha)* Gut reaction?

They go front of stage and start whispering earnestly. Robert, straining to hear, slowly gets up and approaches.

Samantha Can't be a hundred percent at this stage. But I think it's genuine.

Monroe What about the bang on the head?

Samantha Not too serious. Superficial tissue damage. Consistent with a glancing blow from a heavy, flat, metal object - perhaps a... frying pan?

Monroe That's amazing. But it could have caused amnesia - yeah?

Samantha I think so.

Monroe All right. Sixty-four thousand dollar question. Well, ten grand, actually. Is this the man you remember as...*(At this stage, Robert has put his head almost between the whispering couple. Monroe becomes aware of him)* Do you mind?

Robert Do **you** mind! This is me you're whispering about here!

Samantha You'd better come with me.

Monroe Where?

Samantha The hospital. More tests.

Monroe Oh, no. He's not going anywhere.

Samantha All right. I'll have to do the tests here. Sit down please. I'll go and get my bag. Jim, would you mind? I need half an hour or so in private.

Monroe *(slightly hurt)* Oh, right. If you need me, I'll be in my office...with **Mrs** Zebbedee.

Samantha exits.

Robert Oh, so you found her, then?

Monroe Of course. That's how I know who you are.

Robert You're taking her word for it?

Monroe Let's just say, I'm satisfied with the explanations she has given.

Robert Hah!

Monroe Sorry?

Robert Nothing. I just said "Hah!" And I meant it.

Monroe And it has some sort of deep-rooted significance, does it, this "Hah!"?

Robert *(Robert puts up ten fingers tauntingly to remind Monroe of their bet. Monroe pushes out his chin in a gesture of false confidence)* Ten big ones, inspector.

Monroe The only big ones you need worry about, Mr Zeinfeld, are the whoppers you've been telling me for the past two days.

The phone rings, both men look slowly down at it.

Robert She's changed her mind again.

Monroe plucks up courage to answer it.

Monroe Monroe? Yes, Derek. Oh, right. Let's have it then. Right....hang on. *(He suddenly props the phone under his chin, and uses his hands to brusquely examine Robert's teeth)* Right, yeah...back two, right. Which one's that? Left or right? Got it.

Robert decides it's time to enquire what's going on. His diction is somewhat affected by Monroe's probing hands - though we get the message.

Robert Hot hu hok's hoing hon?

Monroe Big one or small one? Hang on. *(Monroe grabs a torch to throw some light on his investigations)* No, that's just some cabbage. Right. Yeah, next. What - the pointy one? Got it. Is that the lot? Thanks, Derek!

Monroe puts down the phone triumphantly, while Robert pulls his mouth back into shape.

Robert What do you want to do next? Check my hooves for stones?

Monroe The appliance of science, my friend. How do you tell if a man is lying through his teeth? Answer - you check his dental records.

Robert Dental records? I thought that was for dead people.

Monroe Why wait? I've just checked your teeth against the records of one Robert Zeinfeld.

Robert And?

Monroe *(leaning triumphantly towards him)* Hah!

Monroe starts heading for the door, as Samantha enters with a kit bag and immediately starts examining Robert's eyes with a lightpen.

Monroe If you need me...
Samantha I won't.
Monroe Right.

A slightly hurt Monroe heads slowly out.

Samantha Look into the light.
Robert What am I around here - a laboratory rat?
Samantha All right. Look forward. Now, this may hurt slightly.

She slaps him hard across the face, timed just as Monroe closes the door.

Robert What the hell was that for?
Samantha That was in case you're lying to me. *(She then grabs his head and kisses him)*
    And that was in case you're not.
Robert I preferred the second one.
Samantha Right, listen very carefully. We…are having an affair.
Robert Are we?
Samantha Yes.
Robert Isn't this a little sudden?
Samantha No, it started six months ago.
Robert Did it?
Samantha Look, I'm sorry about your memory. I feel really bad about it.
Robert Why?
Samantha Because it's probably my fault.
Robert Why?
Samantha Because I hit you with a frying pan.
Robert Why?
Samantha Because we had a row. And don't say "why?"
Robert What about?
Samantha About sex, if you must know.
Robert I must know. Please. I need to know.
Samantha All right. You wanted sex, I didn't. I got tense. You started to sulk. I said I had
    a headache. You said it was a pathetic excuse. I said if you had a headache like mine
    you wouldn't want sex either. You said you would. I said you wouldn't. You said you
    would. I said you wouldn't, and don't you dare say you would. You said you would.
    So I hit you with a frying pan.

Robert Then what?

Samantha Then you had a headache like mine.

Robert But did I still want sex?

Samantha I don't know. You walked straight out through the door and into the night.

Robert And got picked up by the police.

Samantha Sorry. Perhaps we should have had sex.

Robert Oh, come on. I wouldn't have missed this for the world.

Samantha So, has the inspector said anything - about another woman?

Robert He said I was having an affair. But he doesn't know who with.

Samantha Good. For God's sake let's keep it that way.

Robert Why?

Samantha Because I'm married.

Robert I see.

Samantha To the inspector.

Robert No, that's fair enough. *(The information sinks in)* What?!?

Samantha Keep your voice down.

Robert You mean you're his...his...

Samantha The word you're groping for is "wife".

Robert Shit! Shit!! *(Irrational panic)* Does he know?

Samantha Yes. He was at the wedding.

Robert Oh, terrific. That's just wonderful.

Samantha Just stay calm.

Robert Stay calm? Stay...

Samantha Calm!

Robert Do you realize how popular that's going to make me when he finds out?

Samantha He doesn't have to find out.

Robert I knee him in the nuts, go to bed with his wife, and win ten grand off him. I think we can safely say that I'm off inspector Monroe's Christmas list.

Samantha Ten grand?

Robert That hasn't happened yet. But trust me, it will.

Samantha I've told you - he doesn't have to find out.

Robert He's a detective! It's his job to find things out.

Samantha Then let's hope he's lousy at his job.

Robert I think I'm going to be sick.

A Flying Ducks Publication

Samantha Come here. Look, you may have temporarily forgotten about this, Mr Robert
Zeinfeld, but you fancy me rotten.

*Samantha has seductively placed Robert's hands on her breasts.   He stands rather
uncomfortably staring at his rigid hands.*

Robert I do?
Samantha You do. Well?
Robert Well what?
Samantha They're yours.
Robert Are they?
Samantha Yes.
Robert What - both of them?
Samantha Yes. Well, go on.
Robert Go on what?
Samantha Squeeze them!

Robert gulps, then attempts a short, nervous, awkward tweak of her breasts.

Samantha Is that it?
Robert What do you mean?
Samantha Well you are a little bit stiff.
Robert You can tell that from there?
Samantha Never mind. Let's try plan B.

*She sits him down, stands behind him and starts seductively stroking his temples and softly
kissing his brow and ears.*

Robert What are you doing?
Samantha Massaging your memory.
Robert This is a police station.
Samantha So?
Robert It's full of policemen.
Samantha So?

Robert One of them's your husband.
Samantha I know.
Robert What if he comes in?
Samantha He won't come in.
Robert He might.
Samantha He won't.
Robert He might.
Samantha He won't.
Robert He might!
Samantha He won't!

A pause, as she clasps his chin and moves in slowly to kiss him. Robert's reply is muffled by her mouth smothering his.

Robert He might.

Samantha backs off with a sigh. She props the other chair up against the door.

Samantha He won't. Now for God's sake, just...relax.
Robert I'm relaxed.

She again massages his shoulders and moves in for the kiss. Robert is as relaxed as a coiled cobra, his hands tensely gripping the table in front of him. At the vital moment, the phone rings. Robert explodes like a firecracker, grabbing the phone as he leaps up and holding it like it's a bomb. Samantha grabs the phone and answers it.

Samantha Hello? No, he's in his office. It's all right. Bye. *(She replaces the receiver)* So, you're relaxed, are you?
Robert It rang!
Samantha It's a phone.
Robert I'm sorry. I can't do this.

Robert has just picked up the chair from by the door when the door opens and Monroe pops his head in. Robert jumps again and throws the chair down in front of him with a little scream as if it's hot.

Monroe You all right?
Samantha Fine.
Monroe I thought I heard a scream.
Samantha Just part of the therapy. Reliving the experience.
Monroe Oh, right. I'll leave you to it, then.

Monroe exits.

Robert He came in!
Samantha Only because you screamed.
Robert I don't think I'm ready for all this.
Samantha Look, it's very simple. There's only two people in the whole world who know about us - you and me. All we have to do, is keep it that way.

The lights cross-fade to Monroe's office as the phone is ringing. Julia answers it.

Julia Hello? No, I think he went into Interview One. Sorry.

Monroe enters.

Julia How's Robert?
Monroe Tense. And a little confused, which is understandable. For what it's worth, we think the amnesia is genuine.
Julia How do you know?
Monroe Well, Sam seems pretty convinced.
Julia Who's he?
Monroe She.
Julia Oh. Sam's a woman.
Monroe I hope so, it was a church wedding.
Julia She's your wife?
Monroe That's the rumour. She's also a doctor, and she reckons it's genuine.
Julia I'll tell you if it's genuine.

Monroe You?

Julia Just give me two minutes with Robert, and I'll tell you if he's lying or not.

Monroe How can you know?

Julia Because I'm married to him, for God's sake.

Monroe Two minutes?

Julia Thirty seconds. If that.

Monroe Right, you're on. Follow me.

They exit, and the lights cross-fade back to the other side.

Robert So let me get this straight. I've actually...sort of...touched your naked body?

Samantha Yes.

Robert And we've actually...sort of...done it?

Samantha We were like a couple of demented stoats.

Robert I'm beginning to warm to this Zeinfeld business.

The phone rings. Samantha answers it.

Samantha Hello? No, he's not. Well he was in here but he's gone back to his office again. Bye.

She puts the phone down just as Monroe and Mrs Zeinfeld enter.

Julia Hello, Robert.

Robert What do you want?

Julia Have you really lost your memory?

Robert Yes.

Julia Well, let's try and little test, shall we? Do you fancy this woman?

Robert No.

Julia He's lying. I made that just under ten seconds. Anything else I can help you with, inspector?

Monroe That was hardly scientific.

Julia No, but it was deadly accurate. Mark my words, inspector. My husband had a row with his tart, she walloped him with a frying pan, he gets picked up by the police walking the streets, panics, and then makes up some cock-and-bull story about amnesia to cover his tracks.

Robert She's good.

Samantha In my qualified medical opinion, Mrs Zeinfeld, the amnesia is genuine.

Julia This has got nothing to do with medicine, dear, this is about men. Robert is a man, therefore he's a liar.

Robert Oh, and there's the gospel according to Pinocchio.

Monroe Your past record on truth isn't exactly impressive, Mrs Zeinfeld.

Julia That's different. Women usually only lie to get out of a tight hole. Men lie to get into one.

Samantha You know, there is another form of amnesia. A sort of psychological amnesia. Where the patient blocks out something that's just too horrible to remember. I think I've just realized who that something is.

Robert Inspector, please tell me I'm not married to this poisoned gargoyle.

Monroe Well, not for much longer. You're getting a divorce.

Robert Am I?

Julia Damn right.

Samantha Oh, congratulations.

Robert You mean...I'll still be Robert Zeinfeld, but I won't be married to her?

Monroe Correct.

Robert Now that's what I call a happy ending.

Julia Except, of course, you're not Robert Zeinfeld.

A stunned silence.

Robert What?

Monroe Who the hell is he, then?

Julia Bob Smith.

Robert No. No, you can't do this to me!

Monroe Don't panic. She means after the divorce. You're still Zeinfeld. Smith is just your maiden name.

Robert *(to Samantha)* Are you following this?

Julia Boring Bob Smith, the accountant. That's who you were when I found you, and that's who you'll be when I dump you.

A Flying Ducks Publication

Robert I see. And whose idea was the divorce?

Julia Mine, of course.

Robert Does this mean I get lots of money?

Julia Ah, now that depends.

Robert On what?

Julia On Curly.

Robert Who the hell's Curly?

Monroe Hang on a minute. Not Curly O'Rourke?

Julia That's the chap.

Robert Will somebody please explain what's going on?

Monroe Curly O'Rourke's a PI, based in Surrey.

Julia I took the inspector's advice, you see. Hired myself a grubby little Private Detective.

Robert What for?

Julia To find out the name of your tart, of course. She rang for you the other night, by the way. When I answered, she panicked and put the phone down. But I did a 1471 and, guess what? Leicester number. I gave the number to Curly, he said he'd have me photos of your tart by today.

Monroe He'll get them as well. He's a ruthless bastard. *(The door is knocked. Monroe half opens it, and disappears momentarily, leaving Samantha and Robert exchanging looks of panic. Monroe re-appears with a package)* Thanks, Derek. Right. Talk of the devil. Billy Short's just left this package for you in reception.

Robert Oh, good old Billy. How is he?

Monroe You know Billy?

Robert Course I bloody don't know Billy! Who the hell are all these people?

Monroe Billy Short is Curly O'Rourke's partner. Hence the name of their detective agency - Short and Curly's. It doesn't take genius to guess what sort of work they specialize in. Let's have a butcher's, then.

Samantha snatches the package as Monroe goes to open it.

Samantha No!

Julia Oy!

Julia snatches it back. Robert immediately snatches it.

A Flying Ducks Publication

Robert No!

Julia What's going on?

Monroe Hand it over.

Robert You don't want me to do that.

Monroe I do want me to do that.

Robert Trust me, you don't want me to do that.

Samantha He's right, Jim. You don't want him to do that.

Monroe Why not?

Samantha Because it's none of your affair...business. It's none of your business. I mean, it's not really a police matter, is it. It's just between Mrs Zeinfeld and Mr Zeinfeld.

Monroe In that case, let Mrs Zeinfeld have her pictures back.

Samantha No, she can't!

Monroe Why the hell not?

Samantha Because....tell him, Robert.

Robert What?

Samantha Tell him. Tell him why she can't have the photos.

Robert But....

Samantha It's all right. Just tell him the truth.

Samantha has stalked around the back of Monroe and Julia, and is savagely shaking her head as she speaks to inform Robert not to tell the truth.

Robert Because... *(there's a tense moment as Robert struggles to find the appropriate answer)*...because that's not Mrs Zeinfeld.

Samantha Oh, shit.

Robert *(floundering pathetically)* I mean...it looks like her. She's even wearing her clothes. But it's not her. I got my memory back, you see, a few minutes ago. And I know who I am. And I know who she is. And it's not her. It's somebody else. Her real name is....Schrobenhausen. Vera Schrobenhausen. The third.

There's an open-jawed silence.

Samantha Robert?

Robert What?
Samantha That was pathetic.
Robert I was under pressure.

Mrs Zeinfeld makes a grab for the package. Samantha resists initially but is fended off by Monroe. Samantha resigns herself to the worst, as Mrs Zeinfeld opens the package and looks at the pictures inside. There's a tense silence, then she starts to laugh, gently.

Monroe What's so funny?
Julia This is her.
Monroe What?

Samantha grabs a photograph. Monroe instantly snatches it from her.

Samantha It does look like me, doesn't it?
Robert She's certainly wearing your clothes.

Mrs Zeinfeld suddenly attacks Samantha with a blood-curdling scream. The two men leap in to break them apart. There's a short flurry of frenzied activity and noise, which culminates in Monroe holding back a wriggling Mrs Zeinfeld, and Robert doing the same to Samantha.

Samantha She's bloody mad!
Julia You thieving little minx!
Monroe Just shut up! Both of you. Calm down. There's a perfectly innocent explanation
      for all of this.
Robert There is?
Monroe Of course. All right, so I ring Mrs Zeinfeld from home - right? She misses the call
      - dials 1471 - gets my number. Curly tracks the number to my house. He snoops
      around, and takes photos of my wife going to work.
Samantha There you go!
Robert There you go!
Julia Fine. And did you ring me from home?
Monroe No.

A Flying Ducks Publication

Monroe, equally suddenly, now attacks Robert. It starts with a swing punch, which Robert ducks under, and then a general scuffle. The two women do their best to break them up, but can't. In a panic, Samantha looks around for reinforcements, and spots a truncheon. This she brings smartly down onto Monroe's head. Monroe slumps, face-up, unconscious on the floor. There's a stunned silence.

Robert Perfect. That's absolutely ideal.
Samantha He was attacking you!
Robert He was upset with me. And I for one can't blame him.
Julia He needs a doctor.
Samantha I'm a doctor.
Julia I think he needs a more sympathetic doctor.

Samantha examines Monroe.

Samantha He'll be okay. He's just got a bit of a bump on his head.
Julia You don't say? I wonder how that could have happened?
Samantha *(to Mrs Zeinfeld)* Get him a glass of water.
Julia Oh, right. And how are you going to administer it - through a funnel?
Samantha Just do it!

Mrs Zeinfeld exits.

Robert *(shouting after her)* And for God's sake don't tell George what's going on in here! Christ - look at him!
Samantha Don't panic. He's just unconscious, that's all.
Robert Oh, that's all right then! An unconscious policeman. For a moment there I thought it might have been serious.
Samantha I was trying to defend you!
Robert And who's going to defend me in court - Perry Mason?
Samantha You didn't hit him, I did.
Robert Oh, but of course - you specialize in this sort of thing, don't you?
Samantha You're getting hysterical.

Robert Tell me, which is your favourite weapon - the truncheon or the frying pan?
Samantha He's coming round.
Robert Oh, goody. It must be quite handy being able to revive your own victims.
Samantha Will you stop wittering and help me!
Robert How?
Samantha On the chair.

Robert leaps onto the chair.

Samantha Not you! Him!
Robert Oh.

She gets Monroe sitting upright in the chair.

Samantha Where the hell is she with that water?
Monroe Uh. Where am I?
Samantha It's okay, you're at the police station.

Monroe focuses his eyes quizzically on Samantha.

Monroe Who are you?

Samantha and Robert exchange wide-eyed glances. Robert, until that point still cowering pathetically on the chair, suddenly takes his cue.

Robert Erm, Robert, I'm Inspector Monroe of Leicester CID. This is my assistant...George.
Samantha Georgina.
Monroe What am I doing here?
Robert You were picked up this morning by one of my officers. I'm afraid all we know about you is what's in your filofax.

Monroe slowly looks up, and fixes Robert with a stare.

Monroe Nice try, Zeinfeld.

A Flying Ducks Publication

Robert Shit.

Monroe Where the hell do you think you're going?

Robert I'll just go and sit in the cells and rot. It'll save you bothering with the paperwork.

Monroe You went to bed with my wife!

Robert I'm sorry! I didn't know!

Monroe Course you bloody knew!

Robert All right, I knew, but I forgot!

Samantha Don't make a scene.

Monroe I'm sorry? Was that Georgina speaking?

Samantha You shouldn't get stressed like this.

Monroe Oh, and why the bloody hell not?

Samantha I've told you before, it'll make you ill in later life.

Monroe Sod later life. I'm taking my ill health now, while I'm still young enough to enjoy it.

Samantha Look, calm down, and let me explain.

Monroe No, let me explain. Which one of you bastards clobbered me?

Mrs Zeinfeld enters with the glass of water. Robert and Samantha instantly point to her.

Robert/Samantha She did!

Monroe Right! You're under arrest!

Julia I'm already under arrest.

Monroe You're under arrest twice.

Mrs Zeinfeld chucks the water in his face.

Julia Get your own water next time.

Monroe splutters, wiping his eyes.

Robert I'm beginning to feel sorry for this man.

Monroe Mrs Zeinfeld!

Julia Don't tell me, I'm under arrest three times.

Monroe Four times.

Samantha Can I suggest that we all...

Monroe Shut up! You're under arrest as well!

Samantha What?

Monroe You're all under arrest. The whole bloody lot of you!

Robert Do you think he does a discount for block bookings?

Monroe grabs Robert ferociously by the collar.

Monroe You!

Robert I think he means me.

Monroe *(simmering)* Would you think it totally unreasonable of me, Mr bloody Robert bloody Zein bloody feld, if I were to blame all of this on you?

Robert I can see a certain logic in that approach.

Monroe Here I was, happy and naive - new job, fresh start - then you show up.

Robert Sorry about that.

Monroe And what happens? You take every opportunity to make me look a total pillock in front of my fellow officers. You knee me in the nuts. And you steal my wife.

Robert I know, but we're still friends aren't we?

The phone rings as Monroe flattens Robert over the table. It is answered by Samantha.

Samantha Hello?

Monroe Do you realize that with a good lawyer I could kill you and be free within seven years?

Samantha He's a bit tied up right now...

Robert I can see you feel strongly about this.

Samantha What?

Monroe I never want to hear the name Robert bloody Zein bloody feld ever again.

Robert I can understand that.

Samantha *(shocked, putting the phone down)* Jim....

Monroe You have ruined what was mockingly known as my life.

Samantha Jim...

Robert Look on the bright side.

Monroe What bloody bright side?

A Flying Ducks Publication

Robert At least you don't owe me ten grand.
Samantha *(screaming)* Jim!!!
Monroe *(screaming back)* What???
Samantha The police have just picked up a man in Blackpool.
Monroe So what?
Samantha He was severely concussed and half naked. He says his name is…Robert Zeinfeld.

Monroe looks at Robert in disbelief.

Robert You can pay me later.
Monroe It's okay. I'll pay you now. *(Monroe knees him in the groin, then turns to shake hands briefly with Mrs Zeinfeld and Samantha)* Nice meeting you, Mrs Schrobenhausen. And you, Georgina. *(He makes calmly for the door and opens it)* George, take over, would you?

Monroe exits. Samantha runs after him.

Samantha Jim….Jim!

She exits, and the phone rings again. Mrs Zeinfeld answers it.

Julia Hello? *(She covers the mouthpiece and addresses Robert)* George just wants to know if he fell for it.

Robert, doubled over in agony, puts up his thumb and collapses on the floor.
Lights to black.

A Flying Ducks Publication